Football
Facts and Figures

Frances Mackay

1891 football match

Photo credits

The publishers would like to thank the following sources for their kind permission to reproduce the pictures used in this publication.

Action Plus – pages 20, 21
Allsport – cover and pages 2, 6, 7, 12, 13, 14, 15, 16, 23
Mary Evans Picture Library – page 22

Acknowledgements

Thanks to Kevin Massey for help with research.

Published by Hopscotch Educational Publishing Ltd,
29 Waterloo Place, Leamington Spa CV32 5LA
Tel: 01926 744227

© 2001 Hopscotch Educational Publishing

Written by Frances Mackay
Series design by Blade Communications
Illustrated by Dave Burroughs
Printed by Clintplan, Southam

Frances Mackay hereby asserts her moral right to be identified as the author of this work in accordance with the Copyright, Designs and Patents Act, 1988.

ISBN 1 902239 89 X

Contents

Football terms

The player

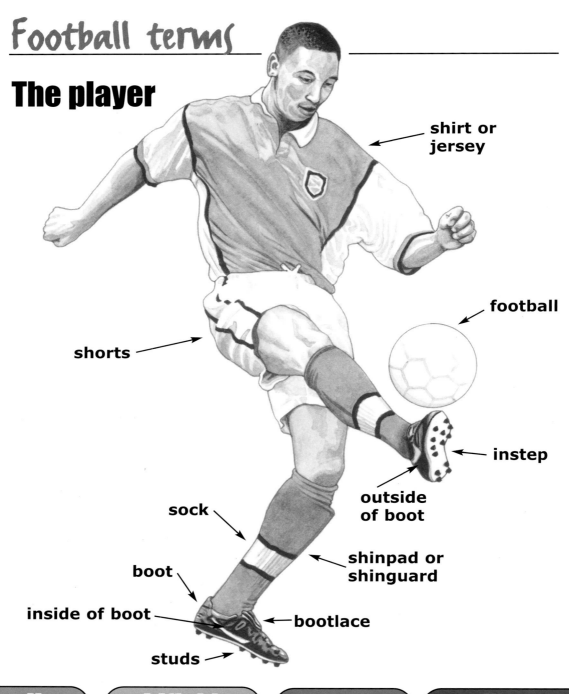

shirt or jersey

football

shorts

instep

outside of boot

sock

shinpad or shinguard

boot

inside of boot

bootlace

studs

striker   midfielder   defender   goalkeeper

Football terms

The game

passing
To pass the ball from one player to another

blocking
To stop the ball from being passed

tackling
To get the ball away from the opponent

shooting
To aim for a goal

volleying
To kick a ball while it is in the air

heading
To hit the ball with the head

feinting
To pretend you are about to turn one way, then turning another

marking
To keep very close to an opponent or to guard an area of the pitch

dribbling
To run with the ball, using the foot to move the ball

receiving
To obtain control of the ball after it has been passed to you

Football organisations

There are many different organisations set up to organise football clubs and competitions. Here are some of them.

FA Cup trophy

FA

The Football Association. The governing body for English football. Organises the FA Cup. The oldest football organisation in the world. Founded in 1863.

UEFA

Union of European Football Associations. The governing body for European football. Based in Nyon, Switzerland. Organises the European Champions League, UEFA Cup and European Championships. Formed in 1954.

FIFA

Fédération Internationale de Football Association. The world governing body. Based in Zurich. Organises the World Cup. Formed in 1904.

The Football League

The body that runs the three English divisions. Organises the Football League Cup. Founded in 1888.

World Cup trophy

The Cup Winners Cup trophy

The Premier League or The Premiership

A league set up for the top English clubs. Founded in 1992.

Scottish FA

The governing body for Scottish football. Organises the Scottish Cup. Founded in 1873.

Scottish League

The body that runs the Scottish divisions. Organises the Scottish League Cup. Formed in 1890.

IFAB

The International Football Association Board. Has responsibility for the rules of the game. Formed by the Scottish, Welsh, English and Irish associations in 1882.

European Cup Winners – 1996. Juventus

Countries that play football

Football is played in nearly every country of the world. FIFA (the world governing body) has grouped them into six areas:

Europe (UEFA)

Albania	Czech	Germany	Netherlands	Slovakia
Andorra	Republic	Greece	Northern	Slovenia
Armenia	Denmark	Hungary	Ireland	Spain
Austria	England	Iceland	Norway	Sweden
Azerbaijan	Estonia	Israel	Poland	Switzerland
Belarus	Faroe	Italy	Portugal	Turkey
Belgium	Islands	Latvia	Republic of	Ukraine
Bosnia-	Finland	Liechtenstein	Ireland	Wales
Herzegovina	France	Lithuania	Romania	Yugoslavia
Bulgaria	FYR	Luxembourg	Russia	
Croatia	Macedonia	Malta	San Marino	
Cyprus	Georgia	Moldova	Scotland	

Central and North America (CONCACAF)

Anguilla	Dominican	Puerto Rico
Antigua and	Republic	Saint Kitts and
Barbuda	El Salvador	Nevis
Aruba	Grenada	Saint Lucia
Bahamas	Guatemala	Saint Vincent
Barbados	Guyana	and the
Belize	Haiti	Grenadines
Bermuda	Honduras	Surinam
British Virgin	Jamaica	Trinidad and
Islands	Mexico	Tobago
Canada	Montserrat	Turks and Caicos
Cayman Islands	Netherlands	United States
Costa Rica	Antilles	US Virgin
Cuba	Nicaragua	Islands
Dominica	Panama	

South Ameri (CONMEBOL)

Argentina
Bolivia
Brazil
Chile
Colombia
Ecuador
Paraguay
Peru
Uruguay
Venezuela

Europe **Africa** **Asia** **Oceania**

Africa
(CAF)

Algeria	Djibouti	Madagascar	Somalia
Angola	Egypt	Malawi	South Africa
Benin	Equatorial	Mali	Sudan
Botswana	Guinea	Mauritius	Swaziland
Burkina Faso	Eritrea	Mauritania	Tanzania
Burundi	Ethiopia	Morocco	Togo
Cameroon	Gabon	Mozambique	Tunisia
Cape Verde	Gambia	Namibia	Uganda
Islands	Ghana	Niger	Zambia
Central African	Guinea	Nigeria	Zimbabwe
Republic	Guinea-Bissau	Rwanda	
Chad	Ivory Coast	Sao Tome and	
Congo	Kenya	Principe	
Democratic	Lesotho	Senegal	
Republic of	Liberia	Seychelles	
Congo	Libya	Sierre Leone	

Asia
(AFC)

Afghanistan	Macao
Bahrain	Malaysia
Bangladesh	Maldives
Brunei	Mongolia
Darussalam	Myanmar
Cambodia	Nepal
China	Oman
Chinese Taipei	Pakistan
Guam	Palestine
Hong Kong	Philippines
India	Qatar
Indonesia	Saudi Arabia
Iran	Singapore
Iraq	Sri Lanka
Japan	Syria
Jordan	Tajikistan
Kazakhstan	Thailand
Korea DPR	Turkmenistan
Korea	United Arab
Republic	Emirates
Kuwait	Uzbekistan
Kyrgyzstan	Vietnam
Laos	Yeman
Lebanon	

Oceania
(OFC)

American	Papua New
Samoa	Guinea
Australia	Samoa
Cook Islands	Solomon
Fiji	Islands
New Caledonia	Tahiti
New Zealand	Tonga
	Vanuatu

South America

Central and North America

Famous clubs

Here is some information about some of the world's most famous clubs.

Arsenal

Arsenal was founded in 1886 in London, England. The club turned professional in 1891. The team's home colours are red and white. The club's nickname is Gunners and some of their most famous players include: Bob Wilson, Charlie George, Liam Brady, Tony Adams, David Seaman, Ian Wright, Denis Bergkamp, Patrick Viera, Emmanuel Petit and Nwankwo Kanu. Arsenal's stadium, Highbury, has a capacity of 38,500.

Bayern Munich

Bayern Munich was founded in 1900 in Germany. Their stadium, Olimpiastadion, can hold 69,256 spectators. Their home colour is all red. Some of Bayern Munich's famous players include: Franz Beckenbauer, Gerd Muller, Sepp Maier, Paul Breitner, Karl-Heinz Rummenigge and Lothar Matthaus. They won the European Cup in 1974, 1975, 1976 and 2001.

Celtic

Celtic, based in Glasgow, Scotland, was founded in 1888. Their stadium, Celtic Park, can hold 60,832 people. Celtic's home colours are white and green hoops. The team's nickname is The Bhoys. Famous Celtic players include: Billy McNeil, Kenny Dalglish, Charlie Nicholas, Paul McStay, Alan Stubbs, Craig Burley, Johan Mjallby, Henrik Larsson and Marc Rieper.

Juventus

Juventus is based in Turin in Italy. Their stadium, Delle Alpi, can hold 71,012 people. Their home colours are black and white stripes but when the club started out they wore red shirts. In the 1930s Juventus won the Italian league championship five times in a row. Famous players include: Gianpiero Combi, Dino Zoff, John and Karl Hansen, Roberto Baggio, Gianluca Vialli and Paolo Rossi.

Liverpool

Liverpool, England, was founded in 1892. Its stadium at Anfield can hold 41,000 fans. Liverpool's home colour is all red. Famous Liverpool players include: Alan Hansen, John Barnes, Kevin Keegan, Kenny Dalglish, Graeme Souness, Ian Rush, Robbie Fowler, Steve McManaman, Jamie Redknapp, Paul Ince and Michael Owen. Liverpool's nickname is Reds or Pool.

Manchester United

Based at Old Trafford (capacity 67,500) in Manchester, England, Manchester United was founded in 1878. Their home colours are red and white. The club was involved in a terrible plane crash in 1958 when eight of their players were killed. It took the club a long time to get over this but they won the European Cup in 1968. Famous players include: George Best, Bobbie Charlton, Denis Law, Ryan Giggs, Eric Cantona, Roy Keane, David Beckham, Andy Cole, Jaap Stam and Dwight Yorke.

Rangers

Rangers are based at the Ibrox Park stadium in Glasgow, Scotland, which has seen two disasters where fans have been killed in 1902 and in 1971. Current stadium capacity is 50,500. Rangers home colours are blue and white and their team nicknames are The Gers or The Teddy Bears. Famous Rangers players include: Bob McPhail, Jim Baxter, Ally McCoist, Paul Gascoigne, Brian Laudrup, Andrei Kanchelskis, Sergio Porrini, Colin Hendry and Giovanni van Bronckhurst.

Real Madrid

Real Madrid is based in Spain at the Santiago Bernabeu stadium that has a capacity of 110,000. The club was founded in 1902. The team's home colours are all white. Real Madrid has won the European Cup in 1956, 1957, 1958, 1959, 1960, 1966, 1998 and 2000. Famous players include: Ricardo Zamora, Santiago Bernabeu, Alfredo Di Stefano, Ramond Kopa, Didi, Jose Santamaria, Pirri, Hugo Sanchez and Emilio Butragueno.

World famous players

There have been many great football players over the years, too many to include in this book, but here are four of the most famous.

Diego Maradona

Maradona was born on October 30th, 1960, in Buenos Aires, Argentina.

Many people consider him to be the world's greatest player during the 1980s and early 1990s. However, he was often in trouble for breaking rules and taking drugs.

1986

He played his first international game in 1977 when he was only 16. In 1980 he was sold to Boca Juniors for £1 million – a record for a teenager. He went on to play for the Spanish club Barcelona and the Italian club Napoli. He helped Napoli win their first Italian League title and the UEFA Cup. He was banned for a while for drug taking in 1991 and again in 1994 when playing for Argentina during the World Cup finals. In 1995 he went back to play for Boca Juniors.

Sir Bobby Charlton

1961

Charlton was born on October 11th, 1937, in Ashington, north-east England.

He is considered by many to be the most famous English footballer of all time. He spent his entire playing career with Manchester United which he joined in 1954 and was only 19 when he played in his first FA Cup final.

He is well-known for his good sportsmanship as well as his excellent playing skills. He played for England when they won the World Cup in 1966 and was European Footballer of the Year in the same year.

He retired as a player in 1974 having scored 247 goals in 754 games. Charlton was knighted in 1994.

Alfredo Di Stefano

1960

Di Stefano is considered by many people to be the best footballer of all time.

He was born on July 4th, 1926 in Buenos Aires, Argentina. He joined the club River Plate in 1943 when he was only 17. He was a very fit player, had excellent player skills and was able to play in any position equally well.

He played for Millonarios in Colombia and Real Madrid in Spain. He was voted European Footballer of the Year in 1957 and 1959.

Di Stefano retired as a player in 1966.

Pele

Pele's real name was Edson Arantes do Nascimento and he was born on October 23rd, 1940 in Tres Coracoes in Brazil.

Pele was a good player from a very young age and he began playing for a local club, Bauru, at the age of 10. He joined Santos in 1956 and at the age of 16 he played for Brazil. In 1958 he became the youngest ever World Cup winner when he scored two goals in the final against Sweden.

Pele played for Brazil at the World Cup in 1962, 1966 and 1970.

Pele retired as a player in 1977 and in 1982 was awarded FIFA's Gold Medal Award for oustanding service to worldwide football. In 1994 he became Brazil's Minister for Sport.

1963

Player awards

Eric Cantona

English Footballer of the Year

1970	Billy Bremmer	Leeds United
1971	Frank McLintock	Arsenal
1972	Gordon Banks	Stoke City
1973	Pat Jennings	Tottenham
1974	Ian Callaghan	Liverpool
1975	Alan Mullery	Fulham
1976	Kevin Keegan	Liverpool
1977	Emlyn Hughes	Liverpool
1978	Kenny Burns	Nott. Forest
1979	Kenny Dalglish	Liverpool
1980	Terry McDermott	Liverpool
1981	Frans Thijssen	Ipswich Town
1982	Steve Perryman	Tottenham
1983	Kenny Dalglish	Liverpool
1984	Ian Rush	Liverpool
1985	Neville Southall	Everton
1986	Gary Linekar	Everton
1987	Clive Allen	Tottenham
1988	John Barnes	Liverpool
1989	Steve Nicol	Liverpool
1990	John Barnes	Liverpool
1991	Gordon Strachan	Leeds United
1992	Gary Linekar	Tottenham
1993	Chris Waddle	Sheffield W.
1994	Alan Shearer	Blackburn R.
1995	Jurgen Klinsmann	Tottenham
1996	Eric Cantona	Man. United
1997	Gianfranco Zola	Chelsea
1998	Dennis Bergkamp	Arsenal
1999	David Ginola	Tottenaham
2000	Roy Keane	Man. United

Scottish Footballer of the Year

1970	Pat Stanton	Hibernian
1971	Martin Buchan	Aberdeen
1972	Dave Smith	Rangers
1973	George Connelly	Celtic
1974	Scotland World Cup team	
1975	Sandy Jardine	Rangers
1976	John Greig	Rangers
1977	Danny McGrain	Celtic
1978	Derek Johnstone	Rangers
1979	Andy Ritchie	Morton
1980	Gordon Strachan	Aberdeen
1981	Alan Rough	Patrick T.
1982	Paul Sturrock	Dundee
1983	Charlie Nicholas	Celtic
1984	Willie Miller	Aberdeen
1985	Hamish McAlpine	Dundee
1986	Sandy Jardine	Hearts
1987	Brian McClair	Celtic
1988	Paul McStay	Celtic
1989	Richard Gough	Rangers
1990	Alex McLeish	Aberdeen
1991	Maurice Malpas	Dundee
1992	Ally McCoist	Rangers
1993	Andy Goram	Rangers
1994	Mark Hateley	Rangers
1995	Brian Laudrup	Rangers
1996	Paul Gascoigne	Rangers
1997	Brian Laudrup	Rangers
1998	Craig Burley	Celtic
1999	Henrick Larrson	Celtic
2000	Marc Viduka	Celtic

European Footballer of the Year

Year	Player	Club
1970	Gerd Muller	Bayern Munich
1971	Johan Cruyff	Ajax
1972	Franz Beckenbauer	Bayern Munich
1973	Johan Cruyff	Barcelona
1974	Johan Cruyff	Barcelona
1975	Oleg Blokhin	Dynamo Kiev
1976	Franz Beckenbauer	Bayern Munich
1977	Allan Simonsen	Borussia MG
1978	Kevin Keegan	Hamburg
1979	Kevin Keegan	Hamburg
1980	Karl-Heinz Rummenigge	Bayern Munich
1981	Karl-Heinz Rummenigge	Bayern Munich
1982	Paolo Rossi	Juventus
1983	Michel Platini	Juventus
1984	Michel Platini	Juventus
1985	Michel Platini	Juventus
1986	Igor Belanov	Dynamo Kiev
1987	Ruud Gullit	Milan
1988	Marco Van Basten	Milan
1989	Marco Van Basten	Milan
1990	Lothar Matthaus	Internazionale
1991	Jean-Pierre Papin	Marseilles
1992	Marco Van Basten	Milan
1993	Roberto Baggio	Juventus
1994	Hristo Stoichkov	Barcelona
1995	George Weah	Milan
1996	Matthias Sammer	B. Dortmund
1997	Ronaldo	Internazionale
1998	Zinadine Zidane	Juventus
1999	Rivaldo	Barcelona
2000	Luis Figo	Barcelona

Michel Platini

Kenny Dalglish

The European Cup

When did it start?

The European Cup (full name: The European Champion Clubs' Cup) was founded in 1955. The idea came from a Frenchman, Gabriel Hanot, who was angry that the manager of Wolverhampton Wanderers claimed that his team were the champions of Europe because they had beaten the strong Honved team from Hungary. Hanot decided to start a new competition to see who were the real champions. It was decided that the competition would begin in the 1955-56 season.

Which teams can enter?

When the competition began, clubs were invited to join and 16 teams entered the first tournament. Today up to three teams from the top countries can enter, plus others depending on their previous performances.

How is the winner decided?

The teams play home and away matches.
The result is decided by the total score, except in the final which is a one-off match.

European Cup Winners. 1984 – Liverpool

Where are the finals played?

The finals are usually played in a venue that is neutral to the two teams.

Which team has won the most times?

Real Madrid (Spain) has won eight times – 1956, 1957,1958, 1959, 1960, 1966, 1998 and 2000. Liverpool is the most successful English club, having won the Cup four times – 1977, 1978, 1981 and 1984.

European Cup Winners

YEAR	VENUE	WINNER	RUNNER-UP	SCORE
1956	Paris	Real Madrid	Stade de Reims	4-3
1957	Madrid	Real Madrid	Fiorentina	2-0
1958	Brussels	Real Madrid	Milan	3-2
1959	Stuttgart	Real Madrid	Stade de Reims	2-0
1960	Glasgow	Real Madrid	Eintracht Frankfurt	7-3
1961	Berne	Benfica	Barcelona	3-2
1962	Amsterdam	Benfica	Real Madrid	5-3
1963	Wembley	Milan	Benfica	2-1
1964	Vienna	Internazionale	Real Madrid	3-1
1965	Milan	Internazionale	Benfica	1-0
1966	Brussels	Real Madrid	Partizan Belgrade	2-1
1967	Lisbon	Celtic	Internazionale	2-1
1968	Wembley	Manchester United	Benfica	4-1
1969	Madrid	Milan	Ajax	4-1
1970	Milan	Feyenoord	Celtic	2-1
1971	Wembley	Ajax	Panathinaikos	2-0
1972	Rotterdam	Ajax	Internazionale	2-0
1973	Belgrade	Ajax	Juventus	1-0
1974	Brussels	Bayern Munich	Atletico Madrid	4-0
1975	Paris	Bayern Munich	Leeds United	2-0
1976	Glasgow	Bayern Munich	St Etienne	1-0
1977	Rome	Liverpool	Borussia M.	3-1
1978	Wembley	Liverpool	Club Brugge	1-0
1979	Munich	Nottingham Forest	Malmo	1-0
1980	Madrid	Nottingham Forest	Hamburg	1-0
1981	Paris	Liverpool	Real Madrid	1-0
1982	Rotterdam	Aston Villa	Bayern Munich	1-0
1983	Athens	Hamburg	Juventus	1-0
1984	Rome	Liverpool	AS Roma	4-2
1985	Brussels	Juventus	Liverpool	1-0
1986	Seville	Steaua Bucharest	Barcelona	2-0
1987	Vienna	FC Porto	Bayern Munich	2-1
1988	Stuttgart	PSV Eindhoven	Benfica	6-5
1989	Barcelona	Milan	Steaua Bucharest	4-0
1990	Vienna	Milan	Benfica	1-0
1991	Bari	Red Star Belgrade	Marseille	5-3
1992	Wembley	Barcelona	Sampdoria	1-0
1993	Munich	Marseille	Milan	1-0
1994	Athens	Milan	Barcelona	4-0
1995	Vienna	Ajax	Milan	1-0
1996	Rome	Juventus	Ajax	4-2
1997	Munich	Borussia Dortmund	Juventus	3-1
1998	Amsterdam	Real Madrid	Juventus	1-0
1999	Barcelona	Manchester United	Bayern Munich	2-1
2000	Paris	Real Madrid	Valencia	3-0
2001	Rome	Bayern Munich	Valencia	2-1

The World Cup

The World Cup was founded in 1930 and is held every four years. The competition is open to any country that is a member of FIFA.

In 1930, the tournament began with just 13 countries taking part (Argentina, Belgium, Bolivia, Brazil, Chile, France, Mexico, Paraguay, Peru, Romania, Uruguay, USA and Yugoslavia). Argentina, Uruguay, USA and Yugoslavia all reached the semi-finals with Uruguay beating Argentina 4–2 in the final.

At the next round in 1934, 16 countries took part – Argentina, Austria, Belgium, Brazil, Czechoslovakia, Egypt, France, Germany, Holland, Hungary, Italy, Romania, Spain, Sweden, Switzerland and USA. Austria, Czechoslovakia, Germany and Italy took part in the semi-finals with Italy winning the final against Czechoslovakia, 2-1.

The following chart gives a summary of further World Cup results.

Year	Qualifiers	Semi-finalists	Winner	Runner-up	Score
1938	Belgium, Brazil, Cuba, Czechoslovakia, Dutch East Indies, France, Germany, Holland, Hungary, Italy, Norway, Poland, Romania, Sweden, Switzerland	Brazil Hungary Italy Sweden	Italy	Hungary	4-2
1950	Bolivia, Brazil, Chile, England, Italy, Mexico, Paraguay, Spain, Sweden, Switzerland, Uruguay, USA, Yugoslavia	Brazil Spain Sweden Uruguay	Uruguay	Brazil	2-1
1954	Austria, Belgium, Brazil, Czechoslovakia, England, France, Hungary, Italy, Mexico, Scotland, South Korea, Switzerland, Turkey, Uruguay, Yugoslavia, West Germany	Austria Hungary Uruguay West Germany	West Germany	Hungary	3-2
1958	Argentina, Austria, Brazil, Czechoslovakia, England, France, Hungary, Mexico, Northern Ireland, Paraguay, Scotland, Soviet Union, Sweden, Yugoslavia, Wales, West Germany	Brazil France Sweden West Germany	Brazil	Sweden	5-2
1962	Argentina, Brazil, Bulgaria, Chile, Colombia, Czechoslovakia, England, Hungary, Italy, Mexico, Soviet Union, Spain, Switzerland, Uruguay, Yugoslavia, West Germany	Brazil Chile Czech. Yugoslavia	Brazil	Czech.	3-1
1966	Argentina, Brazil, Bulgaria, Chile, England, France, Hungary, Italy, Mexico, North Korea, Portugal, Soviet Union, Spain, Switzerland, Uruguay, West Germany	England Portugal Soviet Union West Germany	England	West Germany	4-2

Year	Qualifiers	Semi-finalists	Winner	Runner-up	Score
1970	Belgium, Brazil, Bulgaria, Czechoslovakia, El Salvador, England, Israel, Italy, Mexico, Morocco, Peru, Romania, Soviet Union, Sweden, Uruguay, West Germany	Brazil Italy Uruguay West Germany	Brazil	Italy	4-1
1974	Argentina, Australia, Brazil, Bulgaria, Chile, East Germany, Haiti, Holland, Italy, Poland, Scotland, Sweden, Uruguay, Yugoslavia, West Germany, Zaire	Brazil Holland Poland West Germany	West Germany	Holland	2-1
1978	Argentina, Austria, Brazil, France, Holland, Hungary, Iran, Italy, Mexico, Peru, Poland, Scotland, Spain, Sweden, Tunisia, West Germany	Argentina Brazil Holland Italy	Argentina	Holland	3-1
1982	Algeria, Austria, Argentina, Belgium, Brazil, Cameroon, Chile, Czechoslovakia, El Salvador, England, France, Honduras, Hungary, Italy, Kuwait, New Zealand, Northern Ireland, Peru, Poland, Scotland, Soviet Union, Yugoslavia, West Germany	France Italy Poland West Germany	Italy	West Germany	3-1
1986	Algeria, Argentina, Belgium, Bulgaria, Brazil, Canada, Denmark, England, France, Hungary, Iraq, Italy, Mexico, Morocco, Northern Ireland, Paraguay, Poland, Portugal, Scotland, South Korea, Soviet Union, Spain, Uruguay, West Germany	Argentina France Belgium West Germany	Argentina	West Germany	3-2
1990	Argentina, Austria, Belgium, Brazil, Cameroon, Colombia, Costa Rica Czechoslovakia, Egypt, England, Holland Italy, Republic of Ireland, Romania, Scotland, South Korea, Soviet Union, Spain, Sweden, UAE, Uruguay, USA, Yugoslavia, West Germany	Argentina England Italy West Germany	West Germany	Argentina	1-0
1994	Argentina, Belgium, Bolivia, Brazil, Bulgaria, Cameroon, Colombia, Germany, Greece, Holland, Italy, Mexico, Morocco, Nigeria, Norway, Republic of Ireland, Romania, Saudi Arabia, South Korea, Spain, Sweden, Switzerland, USA	Brazil Bulgaria Italy Sweden	Brazil	Italy	3-2
1998	Argentina, Austria, Belgium, Brazil, Bulgaria, Cameroon, Chile, Colombia, Croatia, Denmark, England, France, Germany, Holland, Iran, Italy, Jamaica, Japan, Mexico, Morocco, Nigeria, Paraguay, Romania, Saudi Arabia, Scotland, South Africa, South Korea, Spain, Tunisia, USA, Yugoslavia	Brazil Croatia France Holland	France	Brazil	3-0

The Olympic Games

The Olympic Games are an international athletics competition held every four years in a selected country. The first modern Olympics were held in Athens in 1896, but the Games actually began in Ancient Greece as long ago as 776BCE.

Football was first played at the Olympics in 1896 as a demonstration sport and again in 1900 and 1904. Football became an official Olympic sport in 1908 when the Games were held in London. The England amateur team won the title.

Hungary has won the Olympic title the most times – in 1952, 1964 and 1968. Three other countries have won it twice: Great Britain (1908 and 1912), Uruguay (1924 and 1928) and the Soviet Union (1956 and 1988).

Romario Farias, Seoul Olympics, 1988

The world's worst football disaster was caused by a decision made at a qualifying match for the Olympics in 1964. Over 300 people died in Lima, Peru, when a riot started after the decision to disallow a last minute goal by Peru in their match against Argentina. The goal would have sent Peru to the Games in Tokyo that year.

In 1996 Nigeria made history as the first African winners who beat the favourites, Brazil, in the semi-final and Argentina in the final.

The Olympic Games

Patrick Mboma, Sydney Olympics, 2000

Year	Venue	Winner	Runner-Up	Score
1908	London	Great Britain	Denmark	2-0
1912	Stockholm	Great Britain	Denmark	4-2
1920	Antwerp	Belgium	Spain	2-0
1924	Paris	Uruguay	Switzerland	3-0
1928	Amsterdam	Uruguay	Argentina	2-1
1936	Berlin	Italy	Austria	2-1
1948	London	Sweden	Yugoslavia	3-1
1952	Helsinki	Hungary	Yugoslavia	2-0
1956	Melbourne	Soviet Union	Yugoslavia	1-0
1960	Rome	Yugoslavia	Denmark	3-1
1964	Tokyo	Hungary	Czechoslovakia	2-1
1968	Mexico City	Hungary	Bulgaria	4-1
1972	Munich	Poland	Hungary	2-1
1976	Montreal	East Germany	Poland	3-1
1980	Moscow	Czechoslovakia	East Germany	1-0
1984	Los Angeles	France	Brazil	2-0
1988	Seoul	Soviet Union	Brazil	2-1
1992	Barcelona	Spain	Poland	3-2
1996	Atlanta	Nigeria	Argentina	3-2
2000	Sydney	Cameroon	Spain	5-3

Football disasters

Unfortunately, throughout the history of football there have been many examples of football disasters. Here are some of them.

1902

25 people died when wooden planking collapsed in the stand at Ibrox Park, Glasgow.

1949

A plane carrying the Italian team, Torino, crashed. 18 of Italy's top players died.

1958

A plane carrying the Manchester United team crashed in Munich. Eight players died.

1964

Over 300 people died in a riot in Peru caused by a decision to disallow a last-minute goal in a match against Argentina.

1971

Disaster again at Ibrox Park when a last-minute goal made departing fans decide to return to the terraces. 66 people were crushed to death.

Ibrox Park, 1902

Football disasters

Flower tributes at Hillsborough, 1989

1985

56 people are burned to death in a fire at Bradford City's stand.

1985

39 people died when a wall collapsed during a riot between English and Italian fans at the Heysel Stadium in Brussels.

1988

Over 70 fans died when a violent hailstorm caused a stampede at a game between Janakpur of Nepal and Mukti Jodha of Bangladesh.

1989

95 Liverpool supporters died at Hillsborough, Sheffield, when they were crushed against a security fence. This led to the decision to have all-seater stadiums.

1996

82 people are crushed to death in a World Cup qualifying match in Guatemala City due to poor crowd control.

Index